THE SCHWEICH LECTURES ON
BIBLICAL ARCHAEOLOGY, 1928

THE OLD AND NEW
TESTAMENTS IN MUSLIM
RELIGIOUS ART

THE OLD AND NEW TESTAMENTS IN MUSLIM RELIGIOUS ART

BY

Professor Sir THOMAS W. ARNOLD

C.I.E., Litt.D., F.B.A.

THE SCHWEICH LECTURES
OF THE BRITISH ACADEMY
1928

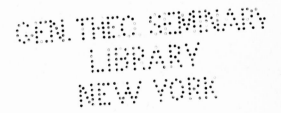
LONDON
PUBLISHED FOR THE BRITISH ACADEMY
BY HUMPHREY MILFORD, OXFORD UNIVERSITY PRESS
AMEN HOUSE, E.C.
1932

OXFORD UNIVERSITY PRESS

AMEN HOUSE, E.C. 4

LONDON EDINBURGH GLASGOW
LEIPZIG NEW YORK TORONTO
MELBOURNE CAPETOWN BOMBAY
CALCUTTA MADRAS SHANGHAI

HUMPHREY MILFORD

PUBLISHER TO THE
UNIVERSITY

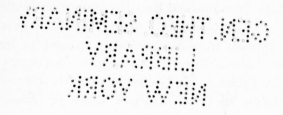
PRINTED IN GREAT BRITAIN

PREFACE

THE posthumous appearance of Sir Thomas Arnold's Schweich Lectures requires a few words of explanation. Although the many claims upon his time prevented him from completing the revision of the manuscript for publication, it was in a sufficiently advanced state to allow of its being printed substantially as it was left at the time of his death in June 1930. There was no indication, however, of the plates which he would have chosen to illustrate the text, and it was necessary to make a selection on the basis of the original slides. Care has been exercised to make the collection of plates as representative as possible of this little-studied branch of Muslim Art, to which Professor Arnold had long devoted special attention, and it is hoped that the volume may form a not unworthy pendant to the masterly survey contained in his *Painting in Islam*. The final revision of the book and the task of seeing it through the press was entrusted to me by the Council of the Academy.

It should perhaps be remarked that the statement made on page 2, that 'no illustrated copy of the Qur'ān is ever known to have existed' may now possibly require to be modified in view of the discovery of a nineteenth-century copy, described by Professor R. Gottheil under the title of 'An Illustrated Copy of the Koran' in *Revue des Études Islamiques* (Paris), 1931, i, 21–4. Although the provenance of the illustrations in this manuscript is still open to doubt, Sir Thomas Arnold would certainly have noted it had he been aware of its existence.

H. A. R. GIBB.

The Council of the British Academy desire to express their profound gratitude to Professor H. A. R. Gibb for the time and trouble which he has devoted to preparing these lectures for the press after the lamented death of their author, to revising the proofs, and to selecting the illustrations. This laborious task was most generously undertaken by Professor Gibb as a tribute to his late friend; and the Council are greatly indebted to him.

CONTENTS

LIST OF ILLUSTRATIONS

THE OLD AND NEW TESTAMENTS IN MUSLIM RELIGIOUS ART

CHAPTER I

IT is one of the ironies of religious history that the Christian Church should have handed on the tradition of its own distinctive art to the rival faith of Islam—and that in the face of the hostile attitude of the Muslim theologians who condemned all such forms of representational art. After the Arab conquest, the Christian Church in the Muhammadan East became depressed under the alien rule of the conquerors, and began to decay in numbers and influence when the support and patronage of the State which it had for centuries enjoyed under the Roman Christian emperors was withdrawn from it; nevertheless, it could still exercise its influence in the realm of art, and hand on to the new society that tradition of Hellenistic culture of which it had so long been the faithful guardian. The appearance in the religious painting of Islam of motives and representations derived from Christian art forms a part of that cultural movement which incorporated in the religious and intellectual system of the Muhammadan peoples Greek learning in its various manifestations— theology, philosophy, medicine, &c. Just as the Christian Church itself had inherited from the earlier religious systems which it displaced artistic conventions to which it gave a religious character, so it now succeeded in passing on this precious inheritance to the new power that had become dominant in the sphere of religion.

Islam has never had a religious art of its own, as a natural outcome of its own religious sentiment or as a means of expressing its religious aspirations. It had from the outset rejected sculpture and painting as means of emphasizing dogmatic truths or of instructing the unlettered in the mysteries of the faith. The builders of mosques were not allowed to include in the decoration of them any sculptures or pictorial representations of the divine story, and no illustrated MS. of the Qur'ān is ever known to have existed; the very idea of such an addition to the sacred text would fill the mind of the pious Muslim with horror. The attitude of orthodox Islam towards the painters found expression in the well-known saying traditionally attributed to Muḥam-mad, that on the Day of Judgement when the painter stands before the Throne of God he will be commanded to put life into the works of art he has created, and when he confesses his inability to do so, he will be forthwith cast down into Hell, as one who had presumptuously dared to arrogate to himself the creative function that belongs to God alone. So firmly rooted and so persistent has been the hostility of the theologians of Islam towards all representational art, that some students of that faith have declared positively that Islam has no representational art whatsoever. But in spite of the judgement of such great authorities as Strzy-gowski, Martin Hartmann, and Ernst Kühnel, the fact remains that there has certainly been a great deal of religious art in the Islamic world, and the growth of it can be traced through as many as seven centuries, in fact, from the thirteenth century—the earliest period in Muhammadan history from which examples of pictorial art have survived to us.

The following problem therefore presents itself: If the ecclesiastical organization of Islam itself, backed by the pre-vailing orthodox sentiment, did not prompt or foster the creation of a religious art, but on the other hand was steadily opposed to any form of activity of this kind, from what sources did such Muhammadan painters, who dared to dis-regard the hostile judgement of the authorities of their own church, derive their inspiration? They had to look abroad, and seek for guidance outside the boundaries of their own religious community. In this attitude of receptivity they showed themselves susceptible to more than one artistic influence, but one of the earliest of which we have clear evidence was that which came to them from the pictorial art of the Christian Church.

In order to understand how this influence became operative, it is important to realize how wide was the extension and how large the numbers of the members of the various Christian churches in the territories included within the Muhammadan empire. For our present purpose we are concerned only with the eastern part of that empire, for any possible contribution to Muslim religious art from Egypt, North Africa, or Spain is uncertain. Since then the first beginnings of Muslim religious art are to be found in Mesopotamia and Persia, let us try to realize what was the extent of the Christian population in those territories at the time of the Arab conquest. As you are aware, this conquest was facilitated by the state of exhaustion to which the rival empires of Rome and Persia had been reduced by the long-drawn-out campaign of Heraclius, protracted through six years between 622 and 627. After the battle of Nineveh in 627 when he finally triumphed over the Persian army, the treaty which crowned his victory restored the boundaries between the empires of Rome and Persia as they had been laid down in the reign of Diocletian. The boundary of Christian Rome ran from north to south through the western part of the great Mesopotamian plain, so that countries which we have long been accustomed to regard as Muhammadan then formed part of the Christian world, and had been ruled by the Christian emperors since the days of Constantine. The various oriental churches which still survive here, though in vastly diminished numbers, Nestorian, Jacobite, Chaldaean, and Melchite, attest the expansion of their ancestors in these regions. But what exactly was the extent of the Christian population at the beginning of the seventh century, when the Eastern provinces of the Roman empire passed under Arab rule, it is impossible, for lack of accurate statistics, to determine. But it must be remembered that Christianity had been the religion of the State for nearly four centuries. The Arab

historians who record the conquest of these provinces de-
scribe the population as Christian with the exception of
scattered groups of Jews. This Christian population were
allowed by the conquerors to retain their faith and continue
the practice of their religious observances, and up to the
period with which we are concerned there is abundant
evidence of their wealth and influence in society. At the
beginning of the tenth century, in the city of Baghdad, the
capital of the Muslim empire, there was a Christian population of between forty and fifty thousand persons, and
monasteries were to be found in almost every quarter of the
city.[1] Towards the close of the same century an Arab geo-
grapher reports that the majority of the inhabitants of the
city of Edessa was Christian, and that they had as many
as three hundred churches.[2] In the early centuries of the
Muslim era, Takrīt, on the right bank of the Tigris and the
northern border of 'Irāq, was almost entirely a Christian
city. The annals of the Crusades bear testimony to the continued existence of the oriental churches under Muhammadan rule; and an acute observer, the monk Burchard of
Mount Sion, writing about 1283, declares that throughout
the whole Muhammadan East, with the exception of Arabia
and Egypt, thirty or more Christians were to be found for
every single Muslim, that is to say, that the Muhammadans
formed only three or four per cent. of the total population.
This estimate certainly appears to be exaggerated, and it
is clear from his language that some of Burchard's contemporaries disagreed with him in this estimate. But he
stoutly maintains it against those who disputed this calcula-
tion, and asserts that he based his conclusions on his own per-
sonal observations and on information derived from persons
acquainted with the facts, as against those who made state-
ments about what they had never seen. We have indeed inde-
pendent evidence that at this period the Christians of Mawṣil
occupied as many as sixty thousand houses in that city.

[1] A. Mez, *Die Renaissance des Islams*, pp. 34–5, 40.
[2] Ibn Hawqal.

If we cross the border into Persia, we find there also a large Christian population, although the religion of the Persian kings, before the Arab conquest, had been Zoroastrianism. In this connexion, especially in any study of the beginnings of pictorial art in the Muhammadan world, it is important to remember that at the period of the Arab conquest the Persian empire extended as far south as 'Irāq and as far west in that region as the borders of its great rival, the Christian Roman empire. The capital itself, Ctesiphon, was also in 'Irāq, and this had been the capital for four centuries; consequently Persian artistic influences were not confined to the diminished Persia of our modern maps, but could make themselves felt in regions extending far to the south and the south-west.

The history of the Christian Church in Persia goes back to the first centuries of the Christian era. The majority of the Persian Christians at the time of the Arab conquest were Nestorians, and the large number of metropolitan and episcopal sees testifies to their vast extension. The Nestorian Patriarch had consecrated a Metropolitan for the Church in China as early as the beginning of the eighth century.

So far from declining in vigour under Muhammadan rule after the Arab conquest, the Nestorian Church entered on that remarkable period of missionary expansion throughout Central Asia, after the Mongol conquest in the thirteenth century had facilitated communications from one end to the other of the vast Mongol empire, stretching from Syria to the shores of the China Sea. The Nestorian Patriarch, Jahballāhā III (1281–1317), had under his jurisdiction as many as twenty-five metropolitans, in Persia, Mesopotamia, Khurasan, Turkistan, India, and China.[1]

The majority of the Christians dwelling in the Eastern provinces of the Muslim empire, with whom we are concerned in this investigation, belonged either to the Jacobite or to the Nestorian Church. Some adherents of the Ortho-

[1] A. Fortescue, *The Lesser Eastern Churches*, p. 98 (London 1913).

dox Eastern Church there certainly were, but their numbers were comparatively few, for they came under the suspicion of the Muhammadan government, as being adherents of the State Church of the Byzantine empire over the border. Further, diversity of race and hostility to the foreign rule of Constantinople had caused the Christian inhabitants of Palestine, Syria, and Mesopotamia to give their allegiance to the Churches which Constantinople regarded as heretical, and consequently the greater part of the Christian population in the East was either Jacobite or Nestorian, and it is in the art of the Nestorians and to some extent in that also of the Jacobites that we must look for the influences that gave rise to the religious art of Islam.

The investigation is beset with great difficulty, for owing to the terrible devastations that have from time to time swept over the territories with which we are concerned, primarily Persia and the great Mesopotamian plain—wars, massacres, and pestilence—all implying the destruction or neglect of perishable works of art, together with the deliberate destruction of all forms of representational art by fanatics—the amount of material that has survived for the student is small indeed. This is true both of the pictorial art of the oriental churches as well as of illustrated books of Muhammadan literature. Churches were destroyed or plundered in great numbers, and few early manuscripts or service-books have survived such destruction or neglect. The same fate has befallen Arabic MSS., and the annals of Muhammadan history are full of stories of the destruction of great libraries by one conqueror and his armies after another; and in this case the orthodox Muslim with his hatred of the representation of living beings has come in to destroy what incendiarism and looting had allowed to survive. Consequently the examples of pictorial art that have survived from the period between the Arab conquest in the seventh century and the thirteenth century are few.

But in order to understand the art of which we find examples in the thirteenth century, it is necessary to take a rapid survey of the circumstances under which artistic activity was possible during the previous six centuries.

The rich and abundant artistic activity of the Orthodox Eastern Church is well known to every student of Byzantine art, and there is no doubt that the ecclesiatical art of both the Jacobite and the Nestorian Churches can ultimately be traced back to Byzantine originals. But the immediate influence of Christian art on Muhammadan painting is undoubtedly derived from those Christians with whom the Muhammadans lived in intimate social relations, who were not only their fellow townsmen, but also in a large number of cases belonged to the same ethnic stock as themselves, namely, the adherents of the Jacobite or of the Nestorian Church, rather than from the art of the State Church of the empire with which the Muhammadans waged at least one campaign every single year.

Further, however strong and persistent may have been the influence of the ecclesiastical art of the Orthodox Eastern Church upon the heretical churches which broke away from it, there were undoubtedly local influences derived from the indigenous art of Mesopotamia and Persia which can be recognized even in the distinctively religious pictures in the service-books of both the Jacobite and the Nestorian churches. Of such specifically local designs I propose to put before you some examples later on. But first I wish to say a few words about such evidence as is available from literary and other sources as to the art which was cultivated by the Jacobites and the Nestorians. Unfortunately the numerous forces of destruction that have overrun Western Asia with relentless monotony throughout the greater part of the Muhammadan era have left but scanty remains of its decorative art. The pictures in modern Jacobite churches are poor and uninteresting, and no examples of an early date appear to have survived.[1] Similarly, modern Nestorian churches are mostly small and

[1] A. Fortescue, *The Lesser Eastern Churches*, p. 344 (London, 1913).

poor,[1] and contain no holy pictures; but this dislike of
pictures on the part of the Nestorians of the present day
appears to be a modern development, possibly a result of
Muslim influence, for in the Chaldaean churches, i.e. the
Uniate churches which were formerly Nestorian, in the
neighbourhood of Mawṣil, there are paintings of saints and
angels made by native artists long before the union with
Rome in the sixteenth century.[2] Similar evidence of such
ecclesiastical decoration in a still earlier period is given in
the story of the dream of a Nestorian Patriarch of the
thirteenth century, in which he went into a great church
adorned with pictures of the Saints, and among them the
Cross.[3] In still earlier and more prosperous times their
churches must have been magnificently decorated, for we
are told that in 759 a Nestorian Metropolitan, Cyprian,
spent as much as 56,000 dinars (i.e. coins of gold) on the
building of a church in Nisibis,[4] and when in 924 the mob
in Damascus plundered a Christian church in that city, the
value of the loot in the form of crucifixes, chalices, censers,
&c. amounted to the vast sum of 200,000 gold pieces.[5]
Equally rich and magnificent must have been the adorn-
ment of the churches built by the Nestorians in Marāgha
(70 miles south of Tabriz), during the period when they
enjoyed the liberal patronage of the Mongol Khans, at the
close of the thirteenth century. We also have evidence of
their artistic activity in the field of secular art. The carpets
of Hīra, once a city with a large Nestorian population,
which was the seat of a bishop up to the end of the tenth
century,[6] appear to have been of Christian workmanship;
elephants, lions, horses, and birds formed part of the patterns

[1] A. Fortescue, *The Lesser Eastern Churches*, p. 145 (London, 1913).

[2] Id., p. 137.

[3] *The History of Jahballāhā III*, translated from the Syriac by James
Montgomery, p. 42 (New York, 1927).

[4] F. Baethgen, *Fragmenta syrischer und arabischer Historiker*, p. 128
(Leipzig, 1884).   [5] Id., pp. 76–7.

[6] Amr b. Mattai, pp. 94–5. (*Maris Amri et Slibae de Patriarchis Nesto-
rianorum Commentaria*, ed. H. Gismondi. Romae, 1899.)

on these carpets, and these designs could hardly have been of Muhammadan origin. The metal-workers of Mawṣil in the thirteenth century, judging from the Christian subjects which they sometimes represented, must also have been, in part at least, Christian.

The discoveries of Professor Herzfeld in the ruins of Samarra have revealed to us in the palace of the Caliph Mu'tasim, built between 836 and 839, paintings of Nestorian ecclesiastics and other representations, and to these the painter has attached a signature which, difficult of interpretation though it may be, seems to indicate that he himself was an adherent of the Nestorian Church. In the throne-room of the palace were found the remains of twelve pillars on which were painted figures of warriors and women and Christian priests. The inscription above the head of the priest has been read by Professor Herzfeld as 'Miflaḥ the sub-deacon', and as it occurs also on paintings of quite a different type, it must be the signature of the painter himself and is not intended to give the name of the personage represented.[1]

Thus in addition to the mosaics and paintings in churches and the illustrations in service-books and other religious works, we have evidence that Christian painters were employed by Muhammadan princes to decorate their palaces. Such decoration was probably not confined to the palace of the Caliph; his example was doubtless followed by the nobles and the wealthy. Most of these, however, have been involved in the same ruin, and little but literary records remain to give us information about them. But, as in other cases, it was probably the Christian painter who was called in to decorate the house of the Muslim noble, and men of wealth in the Christian community also probably had their houses decorated in a similar fashion. This conclusion is suggested by the religious pictures in the house of a Christian citizen of Aleppo, which have been saved from destruction by being transferred to the Kaiser Friedrich Museum

[1] E. Herzfeld, *Die Malereien von Samarra*, p. 91 (Berlin, 1927).

in Berlin. Though these are of a late date, namely the first years of the seventeenth century, as is indicated by an Arabic inscription, there is no doubt that we have here an example of a form of decoration that had been cultivated throughout a long series of previous centuries. The practice of decorating the interior walls of a house with paintings has had a long tradition in the East, and it did not die out in the lands conquered by the Arabs, despite the condemnation of the art of painting by Muslim orthodoxy, and (as already explained) it was in the Christian community that this artistic tradition would be most likely to be kept alive and carried on.

On the wooden walls of this house from Aleppo are painted various incidents from the Old and New Testament, e.g. the sacrifice of Isaac, the daughter of Herodias dancing before Herod, the Virgin Mary and the Child Jesus, Jesus in the Temple, and the Last Supper.[1]

For Persia, there are special circumstances which call for consideration. A strong artistic sense has always been a characteristic of the Iranian peoples, and there is evidence to show that this artistic tradition was kept alive as much by the Persian Christians as by Persian Zoroastrians and those Persians who adopted the faith of the Arab conquerors. In the realm of ecclesiastical art the number of objects exhibiting distinctively Christian workmanship that have survived from the Sasanian period—the period of that national dynasty which governed Persia from 226 up to the Arab conquest in 636—are indeed few, but there are indications that Christian subjects were included among those that were represented. For example, there has survived from the Sasanian period an embossed silver dish covered with such Christian designs as the Denial of Peter, the Crucifixion, the Marys at the Sepulchre, and the Ascension.[2] The majority

[1] F. Sarre, 'Bemalte Wandbekleidung aus Aleppo'. (Berliner Museen: *Berichte aus den Preußischen Kunstsammlungen.* XLI. Jahrgang, Nr. 4, p. 1144 sqq., Berlin, 1920.)

[2] Imperial Archaeological Commission, *Materials for Russian Archaeology*, part 22, vol. ii, p. 44 (1899).

of the Sasanian silver vessels are decorated either with
representations of Sasanian monarchs, either hunting or
enthroned in the midst of cup-bearers and musicians, or
with subjects taken from the earlier incidents of the national
history; but the examples that have survived undoubtedly
form but a very small fraction of those that must at one time
have existed, and since we know that Christian artists took
part in the making of them, these Christian artists must undoubtedly have continued their craft in the Muhammadan
period also. Their activities would have been required for
the decoration of the Nestorian churches, and thus the
Persian traditional method of representing Christian subjects would have been perpetuated just as in so marvellously
persistent a manner incidents connected with the national
epic reappear in Persian painting of the fifteenth and
sixteenth centuries, even though all evidence of their
existence during the intervening period of eight or nine
centuries has been entirely lost.

There is reason for thinking that Christian artists took
part in the production of that charming and attractive
painting which is found on the pottery of Rayy. This city
of Rayy, which in the tenth century was said to have been
the finest city in the whole of the Orient, with the exception
of Baghdad, was situated in the north of Persia not far from
the present city of Teheran. It was plundered and burnt by
the Mongols in the year 1220; it never recovered from that
great calamity, and has remained a ruin to the present day.
From the site of this great city of Rayy come those charming
painted bowls and plates which are familiar to us from the
collections in the British Museum and in the Victoria and
Albert Museum and from illustrated accounts of other collections. Now the city of Rayy contained a considerable
Christian population, and was at one time the seat of a
Nestorian Metropolitan, and though during the eleventh
century it was for purposes of ecclesiastical administration
joined to Hulwān and after 1175, that is, forty-five years
before its final destruction by the Mongols, to the metro-

politan see of Hamadān, a city a little farther to the west, there is no reason to suppose that the Christian community of Rayy ceased to exist. It is almost certain that Christian artists took some part in the production of the decoration of the pottery of Rayy, with its brightly coloured figures of princes, knights, hunters, singing girls, dancers, and musicians, for there is no evidence whatsoever that at this early period, that is before 1220, when this art of Rayy entirely ceased with the destruction of the city, that any Muhammadan artists in this north-eastern part of the Arab empire had ever painted any such figures, so obnoxious to orthodox Muslim opinion.

There must have been a secular art produced by Christian artists, and these Christian artists or their Muslim descendants, carrying on the same methods and traditions, would be ready to work for such Muhammadan patrons as cared to disregard the prohibitions imposed by the Orthodox exponents of their faith. I propose first to put before you examples of this transference of motives and forms of representation, characteristic types of persons, conventional ornamentation and designs, &c., from Christian paintings to the illustration of secular works of Arabic literature, before passing on to the specifically religious pictures which illustrate the subjects taken from the religious literature of Islam.

In the service-books of the Jacobite and of the Nestorian church and in illustrated copies of the Gospels belonging to these churches, we find undoubted examples of the work of painters belonging to one or other of these two churches, and if it can be shown that the same characteristics reappear in illustrated MSS. of works of Muhammadan literature, it then becomes clear that Christian artists, or painters carrying on the same traditional methods as those of the Christians, were employed by the Muhammadan owners of these MSS.; and this transference becomes doubly clear when in examples of Muslim religious art the whole representation, and not details merely, is found to have been transferred from Christian art to Muslim art.

PLATE I

EXAMPLES OF SIMILAR TYPES IN CHRISTIAN
AND MUSLIM MSS. I

But, in the case of the examples of the first class which I now propose to put before you, it is clear that complete transference is impossible, because of the difference in the subject-matter to be illustrated in the two distinct classes of literature—the Christian religious book on the one hand, and the purely worldly writings produced by Muhammadan authors on the other. I will first take examples from an Arabic MS. of the Apocryphal Gospel of the Infancy of Jesus, which is preserved in the Laurentian Library in Florence. It bears the date of the Alexandrian era which corresponds to A.D. 1299 (just about the date of the earliest dated examples of Muslim painting that have survived to us); it was copied in the city of Mārdīn, in the north-west of Mesopotamia just inside the old eastern frontier of the Roman empire. This MS. contains a number of small pen-and-ink outline drawings, of no particular artistic merit, but important for the history of art in view of the early date of the MS. In his representation of the sacred personages whose story is related in the text, the artist has followed the stately tradition of classical art, which was continued in the iconography of the Byzantine Church—tall, solemn, hieratic figures, draped in the severe garments of Greek statuary—such figures as look out of the mosaics of Ravenna and elsewhere. But in the accessories of these illustrations there are many details which closely resemble those we find in Muhammadan MSS., such as common, ordinary folk who sit cross-legged in oriental fashion, and many details of ornament, and patterns woven upon garments, &c. For purposes of comparison we will consider side by side with these features of the Christian MS. similar characteristics to be found in a Muhammadan MS. of much the same date. It is an Arabic translation of some treatises ascribed to a mythical Hermes who is said to have learned from Aristotle the magical properties of metals and precious stones. This MS. bears no date, but the writing and the style of the illus-trations indicate that it belongs to the fourteenth century.[1]

[1] Plate I.

To the thirteenth century belongs that group of pictures which is generally described as belonging to the Baghdad school or to the Mesopotamian school (appellations which it is to be hoped historians of art will soon abandon, because such geographical reference does not draw attention to any of the distinctive features of this group of paintings). A comparison of many of the details of these pictures, which are mostly to be found as illustrations of the *Maqāmāt* of Ḥarīrī, with the illustrations in MSS. of the Gospels or of service-books used in the Jacobite or the Nestorian church, reveals similarities which seem to point to a common origin.[1]

How these influences passed from one religious community to another is a matter of uncertainty. But the determination of the problem becomes more easy if we bear in mind that Christians formed part of the population of every great city in the eastern provinces of the Muhammadan empire ; that a pictorial art of some kind was cultivated among them; and lastly that if a Muhammadan prince or noble wanted to find a painter to illustrate any Arabic or Persian MS. in his possession, such a painter could be found within the Christian community or among such converts to Islam, or descendants of converts, as had kept alive the traditions of artistic activity inherited from their Christian forefathers.

Apart from these details which indicate that Christian painters or the descendants of Christian painters worked for Muhammadan employers in producing these earliest known examples of Muslim painting, we have notable examples of borrowing in the representation of separate incidents of sacred history, e.g. the picture of the Annunciation which occurs on fol. 23 b of the MS. of Rashīd ud-Dīn's *Universal History* in the Edinburgh University Library— a MS. which bears the date A.H. 710 (A.D. 1310–11). In accordance with a tradition common in the Eastern Church, the Angel Gabriel is here represented as meeting the Virgin Mary while she was on her way to fetch water from

[1] Plate II.

PLATE II

EXAMPLES OF SIMILAR TYPES IN CHRISTIAN
AND MUSLIM MSS. II

PLATE III

THE ANNUNCIATION

PLATE IV

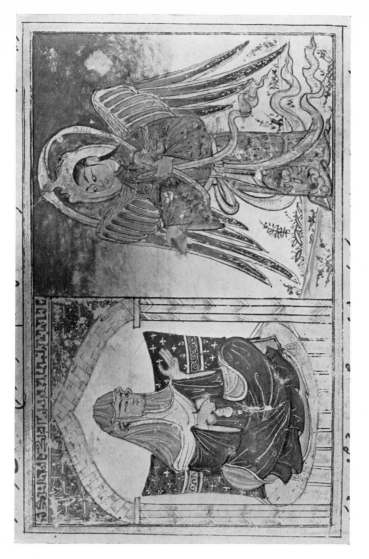

THE ANNUNCIATION

a well; and a comparison of this Muhammadan picture with the mosaic representing the same incident in the church of San Marco in Venice shows that the two artists, though working in cities so far removed from one another as Tabriz in the north of Persia and Venice in the north of Italy, and in periods of time so far removed from one another as the beginning of the fourteenth century and the thirteenth century, derived their particular form of representation from the same conventional type.[1]

Another picture of much the same date, belonging to a MS. dated A.D. 1307 in the Edinburgh University Library, is obviously a copy of some Christian original.[2] It occurs in a treatise on the different systems of chronology current throughout the world, in the course of which the author takes occasion to note the most important anniversaries in the calendar of each country. Accordingly the artist has an opportunity of painting a picture of the Annunciation and has taken a Christian picture as his model. The Virgin is represented as spinning, just as we find her in many Byzantine paintings, but the Muhammadan artist has accommodated the original to the usages of his co-religionists and the conventions of his own time, by making her sit cross-legged on the ground, instead of being seated in a chair.

We have also in a MS. (British Museum Add. 7293, fol. 285 b) of the *Maqāmāt* of Ḥarīrī, copied in A.H. 723 (A.D. 1323), a picture which was clearly originally intended to be a picture of Christ in the midst of the doctors in the Temple.[3] The attitude of the Child and the looks of perplexity and inquiry on the faces of the older men seated around Him all point to such a conclusion. But the artist has transferred this representation to an entirely different story, how a rascally boy whose father had been preaching and exhorting his hearers to show charity to the poor takes advantage of the effect produced by his father's eloquent words, collects money from the congregation, and then goes off with his father to spend it in a wine-shop.

[1] Plate III.　　[2] Plate IV.　　[3] Reproduced in *Painting in Islam*, Plate X.

Another example may be taken from the life of Muḥam-mad in the MS. already referred to (No. 20, Edinburgh University Library) of Rashīd ud-Dīn's *Universal History*. The artist was called upon to depict the birth of Muḥammad. Islamic art provided him with no type to follow, and the Islamic theologians gave him no guidance. He turned therefore to Christian art, and the picture he produced obviously conforms to some Christian original. The angels hovering over the mother of the new-born child conform to a Christian type. In the place commonly assigned to Joseph in Christian pictures of the Nativity sits ʿAbd al-Muṭṭalib, the grandfather and guardian of Muḥammad, who was a posthumous child. On the opposite side of the picture the three women who are coming to visit the mother occupy the place that would have been assigned to the three Wise Men in any Christian painting.

CHAPTER II

IN the last chapter we considered the circumstances which seem to point to the conclusion that religious art in Islamic painting derived its origin from representations of similar subjects in Christian painting. The two religions had taken over from Judaism stories of sacred history that had much in common, and Islam accepted Jesus as one of the prophets of God. It was only from Christian art that any guidance could be obtained in regard to the pictorial representation of these stories, for the accepted religious teachers of Islam not only offered no assistance to the painter, but on the contrary were entirely hostile to his activities, and consequently made no effort to build up a traditional form of Islamic religious painting. Further, a comparison of some of the earliest examples of religious art in Islam appear to indicate that when Muhammadans, despite the disapproval of the leaders of their faith, felt a desire for some pictorial representation of their own religious history, they employed either Christian artists or such Christian converts to Islam as had carried with them into the new society they had joined the traditions of their ancestral craft. But in succeeding centuries, according as painting received a more generous patronage, and the artists worked under the protection of sultans and powerful nobles, especially those of Persian, Mongol, or Turkish stock, the Muhammadan painters freed themselves from such leading-strings and used their own imagination in inventing for themselves various ways of depicting such stories of the Old and New Testament as formed part of the sacred literature of Islam.

But before entering upon a detailed examination of the varied manner in which the Muhammadan painters dealt with the problem with which they were faced, it is important to recognize what place these pictures filled in the religious life of the Muslim world. As already explained, such paintings as we shall study could never win the com-

D

mendation of the ecclesiastical authorities of Islam, because of the condemnation of all forms of representational art by the theologians and the general body of the orthodox. No pictures could be painted for a mosque or for any building in which devotional exercises took place. The Muslim painter consequently pursued his craft with a consciousness of the disapproval of his efforts on the part of all devout persons; he could never feel, like the Christian painter, that pious persons would kneel and pray before his picture, and that it might stimulate the tears of the penitent or the aspirations of the godly; least of all could he, like Fra Angelico, kneel at his work as at a service well pleasing to God. His task was rather that of an illustrator of books, and consequently the paintings that represent incidents from religious history are often found side by side in the same volume with others of a purely secular character. They are never intended to give visible form to some dogma of the faith, or to stimulate devotion. They form part of the art of illustration.

To pass now to the subject-matter of these pictures.

Every student of Islam knows that a large part of the contents of the Qur'ān is derived from the Old Testament, and to a lesser degree from the New Testament. The stories told of various familiar Biblical personages are, from our point of view, somewhat strangely selected, and appear to be introduced mainly with the object of emphasizing the doctrine of God's relationship to man as communicating His will through the medium of Prophets, and of giving warning of the punishment that falls upon those who reject the divine message thus communicated and are guilty of the sin of idolatry.

Beginning with Adam and Eve and their expulsion from Eden, we have the story of the death of Abel; several references to Noah and his ark, and the destruction of unbelievers in the Deluge; long accounts of Abraham, whom Muḥammad represented as the builder of the Ka'bah in Mecca and as the progenitor of the Arabs through Ishmael; Jacob, and his son Joseph, whose story is told at greater length and with more abundant detail than that of any other Prophet, except Moses; of David there is only a brief mention; his son Solomon, however, receives a long notice, especially in connexion with the visit of the Queen of Sheba; a few verses are devoted to Job, and to Jonah, but Elijah and Elisha and Ezra are merely mentioned by name. Thus large sections of Old Testament history are left out altogether; only a small part of the story of the early patriarchs is brought in; the period of the Judges is passed over unnoticed, and no account is given of the history of the kingdoms of Israel and Judah after the death of Solomon. Of Isaiah and other Prophets of the Old Testament there is no mention at all. Even within the narrow limits of this choice of personages, the narration of incidents is curiously selective. But while there are the briefest possible references to events related at length in the Old Testament, on the other hand many incidents are added which can be traced to an external source, either to the Talmud or Midrash.

All these stories provided abundant material for the painter to illustrate—not that he was ever given an opportunity of bringing out an illustrated edition of the Qur'ān, for such a work would have appeared to Muslim sentiment so blasphemous as to be absolutely inconceivable. So we should look in vain for Muslim religious pictures in such places as we are accustomed to find Christian pictures—in a house of prayer or in the pages of the Word of God. But there are numerous other writings in which these same stories are repeated, and these provided material for the painters to illustrate. Such works were the *Stories of the Prophets*, and several compositions by different authors are extant under this title; they reproduced with considerable amplification the narratives given in the Qur'ān, adding, of course, a life of Muḥammad himself. Further, works of secular history, recounting the annals of monarchs and kingdoms of comparatively recent date, were frequently prefaced by a summary of the history of the world from

Adam upwards, just as the Rabbi Joseph writing in the sixteenth century *The Book of the Words of the Days of the Kings of France and the Kings of the House of Othman the Turk* begins his chronicles with the words 'Adam begat Seth and Seth begat Enoch', and Christian chroniclers in the Middle Ages often gave similar summaries of the history of the world before they settled down to record the events of their own time. Moreover, these stories of sacred history, contained in the text of the Qur'ān, the revealed Word of God, formed an integral part of the common thought of the Muslim world, for it must be remembered that some part or other of the Arabic text of the Qur'ān must be repeated by the faithful during each of the five times of divine worship, every single day of their lives; the Qur'ān is the first book which the boy begins to study, and it should be familiar to every cultivated Muslim. Accordingly the stories contained in it were made use of by the poets, especially by the authors of didactic or mystical writings, in order to illustrate some particular thought or emphasize some point of doctrine, while certain stories, particularly that of Joseph, were taken as the subject-matter of romances, either in prose or verse. Consequently, as the Muhammadan world does not draw the same rigid line between the religious and the secular as we find in Christendom, but intermingles religious considerations with almost every single aspect of life and thought, the religious art of the Muhammadan world was not relegated to a place apart, but made its appearance, in the form of illustration, in compositions of the most diverse character.

As already explained, in dealing with this material the Muslim artist had no tradition on which to base his own peculiar form of representation, except such as Christian religious art could give him. When, therefore, the Muslim painter ceased to copy Christian models, he was obliged to follow his own devices, and his illustration of any religious incident generally corresponded in design and character to those of the particular secular subject that he might be

called upon to deal with.   The work of the Muslim painter
varies in consequence according to the particular degree of
attainment reached by the contemporary art of his own
country and time, but it is a matter of regret that the
greatest artists in the annals of Islamic painting have left us
few specimens of their work that can be described as belonging to religious art.   The examples, therefore, that I have
to put before you are for the most part of less interest from
the point of view of artistic excellence than from that of the
subject-matter.

The series of the Prophets of Islam begins with Adam.
The Christian world is accustomed to representations of
Adam and Eve as naked, but in Muslim art examples of
the nude are exceedingly rare, and respect for one of the
Prophets of Allah probably stood in the way of a Muslim
painter so far outraging orthodox sentiment as to paint him
naked.   In one picture we find Adam and Eve arrayed in
long white shirts, like the shirt with which Eve is being clad
in the mosaic which presents the story of the Creation and
the Fall in the vestibule of St. Mark's in Venice; and since
these mosaics were executed by workmen sent from Constantinople, who followed the traditions of art in the
Oriental Church, we probably have in this Muhammadan
picture a survival of the same tradition, though the MS.
from which it is taken is so recent as the end of the sixteenth
century.   A rare example of Adam and Eve, represented as
partly nude, occurs in a Persian anthology compiled in
1410 for Sultan Iskandar, a grandson of Timur, who
reigned in Iṣfahān, the MS. of which is now in the possession
of Mr. Gulbenkian.

Another example probably goes back to a Christian
original, intended to represent God as walking in the
garden of Eden with Adam and Eve, but the Muhammadan
artist who in A.D. 1307 made use of this picture for the purpose of illustrating a MS. of a work by al-Beruni on the
various systems of chronology in the world (Edinburgh
University Library, Arabic No. 161, fol. 49 b) has slightly

transformed the picture to suit his own purpose.[1] He wished
to illustrate the Zoroastrian legend of the temptation of the
first man and woman (Mesha and Meshyana); they are said
to have lived happily on earth for fifty years without any
need of eating or drinking, and free from all pain and
sorrow. Then Ahriman, the Spirit of Evil, appeared to
them in the guise of an old man and persuaded them to eat
of the fruit of the tree. He set them an example, and in this
picture he is represented as holding a pomegranate in his
hand, and as soon as he ate of it, his form was changed into
that of a beautiful youth. Meshyana, who in this picture is
holding in her hand an apple, was so struck by the trans-
formation that she followed his example and thus fell from
her primitive high estate. No representation of this incident is known to exist in Zoroastrian art, and the changes
necessary for the Muhammadan artist to adapt some Christian picture to his own particular purpose were slight.

A more typical Muhammadan representation of Adam
and Eve in the Garden of Eden, in which the artist has
shaken himself free from all traditions and has followed his
own fancy to the extent of arraying these holy personages in
the costume of his own time (the seventeenth century)
occurs in a MS. (of that date) of the *History of the World* by
Mīrkhwānd.[2] The figure in the lower left-hand corner is
intended to represent the Devil in disguise, holding out an
apple in his right hand; but the face is much damaged and
has been disfigured by a clumsy attempt at restoration.

The Muhammadan compilers of the *Stories of the Prophets*
enlarged considerably upon the story of Adam and Eve as
given in the Old Testament and the Qur'ān, and also upon
that of their children, Cain and Abel. The murder of Abel
is rarely represented, but occurs in a MS. of the sixteenth
century of a *History of the Prophets* by Isḥāq ibn Ibrāhīm al-
Nīshāpurī; it was once in the Imperial Library of Delhi and
is now in the Bibliothèque Nationale (Supp. persan 1313,

[1] Plate V.
[2] Bibliothèque Nationale (Suppl. persan 1567, fol. 14 b).

PLATE V

ADAM AND EVE
(MESHA AND MESHYANA)

PLATE VI

CAIN AND ABEL

PLATE VII

NOAH

fol. 15).[1] The text relates how the Devil killed a snake by breaking its head with a stone in the presence of Cain, and thus suggested to him the way in which he might slay his brother, and Cain finding Abel asleep under a tree killed him in the manner indicated. From the Midrash was borrowed the story of Cain's perplexity as to what he should do with the dead body of the brother whom he had murdered, and he carried it about on his back until God sent a raven which scratched up the earth with its bill in order to bury another raven that had died, and thus indicated to Cain the proper method of human burial. The Qur'ān, however, slightly alters the story as found in Midrash, for the latter states that it was Adam who first saw the raven and buried the body of Abel after the same fashion. The Muhammadan narrator goes on further and tells how Adam and Eve mourned so bitterly over the death of their younger son that God took pity upon them and allowed Abel to return to his parents for the space of twenty-four hours. In an illustration of this incident which occurs in a MS. dated 1307 in the Edinburgh University Library (Arabic No. 161, fol. 122 b) we see that Adam and Eve have prepared an abundant feast in order to welcome the son thus for a brief space restored to them.

The Ark of Noah is frequently represented, and the Muhammadan painter is as much embarrassed as was his Christian confrere in his efforts to resolve the problem of what to do with the animals when he had got them safely into the ark. In this picture, from a MS. in the British Museum (Add. 18576, fol. 19 b),[2] the artist has settled the problem by opening the sides of the vessel so as to reveal the animals packed away in the hold, while Noah and the members of his family are safely seated on the deck. The rising waters of the deluge surge around them, and must originally have been painted in silver, but, as is the case in all these pictures, the silver has become tarnished and is now quite black. The young man clinging to the minaret, which

[1] Plate VI   [2] Plate VII.

is about to be engulfed in the rising waters, is Canaan, who is said to have rejected his father's warning and perished along with the wicked in consequence.

In a MS. dated A.H. 933 (= A.D. 1527) of a Persian translation of the *Zoological Dictionary* of Damiri, the artist has contented himself with four animals merely, a lion, an ox, a deer, and a panther, which are seated on the deck of an exact representation of a sailing-vessel of the early part of the sixteenth century. Noah is seated on the high poop, while the dove is flying away from the bow of the ship.

In accordance with the important place given to Abraham in the Qur'ān, pictures of him are fairly common, especially as the Persian poets often introduce incidents from his biography into their narratives. But the Qur'ānic account of Abraham, ample though it is, follows Midrash much more than the Old Testament and narrates at length the story of how Abraham smashed his father's idols. In the Edinburgh MS. of al-Beruni's *Systems of Chronology* (Arabic No. 161, fol. 102 b) he is thus shown as having knocked them down with an adze. When this sacrilegious destruction is discovered Abraham is brought before King Nimrod, who condemns him to be burnt to death. An enormous fire of wood is kindled, but the heat of the flames is so tremendous that no one can approach it. Accordingly Abraham is hurled into the midst of the flames by means of a catapult. In the MS. of Mīrkhwānd's history already referred to[1] Abraham is shown clinging somewhat insecurely to the bowl of what at first appears to be an enormous spoon which is being let down by means of a rope in such a way as to drop the Prophet into the midst of the flames, while an angel swoops down from Heaven in order to assist the Prophet in his perilous descent.

In another MS. belonging to a previous century, the Prophet is seen seated in the midst of the flames which the artist has only partially represented, in order to be able to show that God has made a space in the middle of them, so

[1] Bibliothèque Nationale (Suppl. persan 1567, fol. 40); see Plate VIII.

PLATE VIII

ABRAHAM

cool that the grass and flowers have sprung up and a stream of fresh water has gushed out from the earth. Indeed Abraham is reported to have told a friend afterwards, that never in his life had he suffered so intensely from cold as when he was sitting in the midst of this fire. The angel whom God has sent to comfort him is kneeling on the grass at his side, while King Nimrod in astonishment surveys the scene from a safe distance at the top of a minaret.

The obedience of Abraham in being ready at the command of God to sacrifice his son is also taken as a subject of pictorial representation by Muslim artists, but does not appear so frequently in their work as in that of Christian painters. The name of the son who was to be the victim on the occasion of this sacrifice is not given in the Qur'ān, and the Muhammadan commentators are not agreed as to whether it was Isaac or Ishmael, though the majority of them incline towards the latter opinion. But Ishmael is distinctly named as assisting his father in building the Ka'bah, the Holy House in Mecca. 'And We commanded Abraham and Ishmael, Purify My house for those who shall go in procession round it and those who shall abide there for devotion and those who shall bow down and prostrate themselves' (ii, vv. 119, 121).

This story, as being so closely connected with the central point of the yearly pilgrimage which attracts so great a body of the faithful to Mecca from all parts of the Muhammadan world, has often been painted by Muslim artists, and there is a great number of pictures of Abraham and Ishmael standing in prayer before the newly erected edifice.

But of all the great personages of the Old Testament none has stirred the imagination of the Muhammadan world so profoundly as Joseph, and none of the Prophets of Islam receives pictorial treatment so frequently as he. The explanation of this is to be found in the large place which the story of Joseph fills in Islamic literature. The Qur'ān devotes a whole chapter to him, which is called after his name, and not only is his story included in the various compilations of the histories of the Prophets, but it was made the subject of separate compositions both in prose and poetry in the different literary languages of the Muhammadan world. Of these the best known is the poem by one of the earliest and the greatest of Persian writers, Firdawsī, whose epic poem *Yūsuf and Zulaykhā* was written about the year 1010, when the poet was already more than seventy years of age. But even Firdawsī had had two predecessors among Persian poets who chose this subject, and later on an enormous number of imitators. Among the latter was the famous poet Jāmī, who strangely enough like his illustrious predecessor had already reached the age of seventy when, in 1483, he composed the poem which takes rank among the greatest achievements of Persian poetic genius. Nine years after the completion of Jāmī's romance, the Turkish poet Ḥamdī completed his own popular poem, which is still regarded as the finest presentation of this theme in Turkish poetry, though many other Turkish poets in succeeding generations took up the same subject. Similar poems were written in other languages of the Muhammadan world. This vast literature, including many widely read and popular poems, has provided the painters with ample opportunity for illustration, and it is only possible here to draw attention to a few examples. A charming picture of Joseph as a boy, meeting a shepherd, while he is on his way to find his brethren, occurs in a MS. of Jāmī's *Yūsuf and Zulaykhā*, dated A.D. 1474.[1] In a MS. of a later date (sixteenth century) of Firdawsī's poem, Joseph is seen being let down into the well, at the bottom of which stands an angel who catches him so as to break his fall, for his brothers at the mouth of the well have cut the rope by which he was suspended. In a MS. in the British Museum (Or. 4535) we see him being drawn out of the well (fol. 60 b) and, later, escaping from Potiphar's wife (fol. 96).[2]

[1] Bibliothèque Nationale (Suppl. persan 561, fol. 84b); see Plate IX.
[2] Plate X. For other illustrations of the story of Joseph see *Painting in Islam*, plate XXXII and p. 107.

PLATE IX

JOSEPH AS A BOY

PLATE X

JOSEPH AND ZULAYKHA

More than double the space allotted to Abraham in the Qur'ān is devoted to the story of Moses. Chapter xxviii begins: 'We will recite unto thee of the history of Moses and Pharaoh with truth for the teaching of those who believe.' Accordingly the sacred text tells the familiar tale of the slaughter of the male children of the Israelites by King Pharaoh—how the mother of Moses set her baby afloat in an ark and how he was rescued by the wife of Pharaoh, who hands him over to his own mother to be reared. Then follows the story of his slaying the Egyptian who was maltreating an Israelite and of his flight into Madian, where he waters the sheep of the daughters of Shu'aib (as Jethro is called in the Qur'ān). Moses is then hired to tend the sheep of Jethro, and after his marriage to the daughter of Jethro he has his vision of the Burning Bush and receives the promise of the company of Aaron in his interview with Pharaoh. When he demands of the king the release of the Children of Israel and Pharaoh calls upon him to produce a sign as proof of his mission, he throws down his staff which becomes a serpent and swallows up the serpents of the magicians. Still Pharaoh refuses to release the Children of Israel, until after the Plagues are sent upon Egypt, and when the Children of Israel have crossed the sea, the waves overwhelm Pharaoh and his host. During their wanderings in the desert, God provides for them manna and quails to eat, and Moses strikes the rock with his rod so that the waters gush out and the people drink. While Moses is absent on Mount Sinai, the Israelites worship the calf, and when he returns to them bearing the tables of the Law, he upbraids them for their return to idolatry and burns the calf until it is reduced to powder, which he scatters in the sea. When the Israelites were unwilling to accept the Law, God is said to have lifted Mount Sinai over their heads until they repented. Then the Israelites wander in the desert for forty years. When Korah and his company rebel against Moses they are swallowed up in the earth.

In all this, the Bible narrative is more closely followed

than in the majority of the stories taken from the Old
Testament, though it is true there are some deviations and
certain additions are made.

Of all the various incidents in this long story, the one most
frequently selected by the Muslim painters is that of the rod
of Moses which became a serpent. It is shown here from a
MS. of the sixteenth century in the Bibliothèque Nationale
(Suppl. persan 1313, fol. 79 b).[1] The rod of Moses, having
been turned into a dragon of terrific appearance and gigantic
dimensions, has apparently already swallowed the serpents
produced by the rods of the magicians of Pharaoh, and has now
turned upon the magicians themselves. One is lying dead at
its feet and it is threatening another with its fiery breath.
This picture bears the signature of one of the most famous
of Persian painters of the sixteenth century, Āqā Rizā.

In the corresponding picture in Mr. Chester Beatty's MS.
of the *Stories of the Prophets*, the dragon is swallowing one of
the magicians, and even Moses himself seems to be alarmed
at the sight of the monster, and Pharaoh looks on from a safe
distance on the other side of a hill.

The descent of Moses from Mount Sinai and the un-
willingness of the Children of Israel to accept the new Law
is illustrated in the MS. of the seventeenth century of
Mīrkhwānd's *History*.[2] In this the Angel Gabriel is represented as holding the mountain over their heads while they
crouch in terror and repentance beneath it.

The punishment that falls upon Korah and his company
is pictured in the MS. of Rashīd ud-Dīn's *Universal History*
in the Edinburgh University Library (Arabic No. 20),
A.D. 1310. It is a dramatic presentation of the story,
and Korah appears to retain his threatening attitude towards Moses right up to the end. The strange object behind him probably represents his palace, for the Qur'ān
says that God caused the earth to swallow up Korah and
his palace (xxviii, *v.* 71).

[1] Plate XI.
[2] Bibliothèque Nationale (Suppl. persan 1567, fol. 108 b).

PLATE XI

MOSES AND THE MAGICIANS

In the history of the Old Testament after the time of Moses Muḥammad appears to have taken very little interest. Saul receives a passing mention in the Qur'ān and he collects an army to fight against Goliath. 'And when they went forth against Goliath and his forces they said, "O our Lord pour out upon us patience and set our feet firm and help us against the unbelievers". And by the will of God they routed them, and David slew Goliath' (ii, vv. 251–2). But this is the only incident in the life of David that received explicit mention. There appears to be some remote allusion to the story of David and Bathsheba, for the parable of Nathan about the rich man who had many flocks and herds and the poor man who had only one little ewe lamb occurs under the form of a dispute between two shepherds who submit their case to David for his decision; but neither Nathan nor Bathsheba are mentioned by name.

The picture of David therefore presented in the Qur'ān is rather vague and indefinite, and is summed up in the following verses: 'God gave him the kingship and wisdom, and taught him according to His will' (ii, v. 252); 'Higher gifts have We given to some of the Prophets than to others, and the Psalter We gave to David' (xvii, v. 57); 'And We constrained the mountains and the birds to join with David in our praise, . . . and We taught David the art of making mail' (xxi, vv. 79–80).

In all this there is little material to attract the artist except the fight between David and Goliath, and even this is but seldom represented (though a picture of it occurs in quite an early MS. dated A.D. 1388 of an anonymous work on *The Marvels of Creation*[1]), probably because in the thought and literature of Islam David has never filled the prominent place which he has taken in the mind of Christendom.

On the other hand, his son Solomon is a familiar figure both in art and literature. The Qur'ān devotes as much space to him as to Abraham, and tells at length the story of his relations with the Queen of Sheba. God is said to have

[1] Bibliothèque Nationale (Suppl. persan 332, fol. 99 b).

subjected unto Solomon the wind and the devils who dived
for him into the sea, and armies of jinns and birds, and
bestowed upon him knowledge of the language of the birds.
With the assistance of the jinns he was able to make 'lofty
halls and images and large dishes like great tanks for water-
ing camels, and cooking-pots that stood firmly' (xxxiv, v.
121). Later writers considerably amplify the story of his
miraculous powers and the romantic story of the visit of the
Queen of Sheba. In Persian art from the sixteenth century
onwards, as also in the Indian paintings which took it as
a model, it became common to insert in the frontispiece of
books of poetry a picture of Solomon enthroned, with the
Queen of Sheba by his side, surrounded by birds and
animals and jinns and all kinds of strange fantastic monsters.
In the delineation of these the painter allowed his imagination to run wild, as in an example from the Museum of Fine
Arts, Boston. In early examples of such pictures the artist
may impose upon himself a certain degree of restraint as in
the MS. of *The Marvels of Creation*, dated 1388, already
referred to.[1] This MS. was copied for the library of Sultan
Aḥmad ibn Uways, the Jalāir Sultan of 'Irāq (1382–1410),
whose magnificently illustrated *Diwan* has recently been
published in facsimile by Dr. F. R. Martin. The personage
kneeling in the foreground is the wise minister of Solomon,
Āṣaf. What is the significance of the fish which seems about
to jump into a metal vessel is uncertain.

Of the well-known story in the Qur'ān telling how the
Queen of Sheba did not recognize that glass had been laid
over the stream of water running through the garden of
Solomon's palace, it is not necessary to give any illustration
here, as one of the most beautiful representations of it in a
MS. in the Bodleian Library[2] has already been reproduced
in my book *Painting in Islam*.[3]

Of later personages in the Old Testament there is little
more than a bare mention of their names in the Qur'ān,

[1] Bibliothèque Nationale (Suppl. persan 332, fol. 5).
[2] Ouseley Add. 24, fol. 127 b.   [3] Plate XXXIII.

PLATE XII

JONAH AND THE FISH

thus providing no material for the artist to work upon, with the exception of Jonah and Job. Of the former the Qur'ān says:

'Jonah too was one of the apostles, When he fled unto the laden ship, And lots were cast and he was doomed, And the fish swallowed him, for he was blameworthy. But had he not been of those who praise Us, In its belly he had surely remained till the day of Resurrection. And We cast him on the bare shore—and he was sick; And We caused a gourd plant to grow up over him' (xxxvii, vv. 139–46).

The fish of Jonah commonly occurs in Muslim art, but is nowhere so finely depicted as in the MS. of Rashīd ud-Dīn's history in the Edinburgh University Library (Arabic No. 20, fol. 25).[1] The author of this vast historical work was still alive when this MS. was copied and it is probably one of those which he had prepared for his own use or for distribution to contemporary Muhammadan monarchs. There is evidence that he summoned artists from different countries, and the choice of a carp as the fish that swallowed Jonah would seem to indicate that this picture is either the work of a Chinese artist or of some painter working under Chinese influence.

The story of Job is only briefly stated in the Qur'ān, where it is written: 'When he cried to his Lord, "Truly evil hath touched me: but Thou art the most merciful of those who show mercy." So We heard him and lightened the burden of his woe; and We gave him back his family and as many more with them' (xxi, vv. 83–4). Another chapter of the Qur'ān adds an incident which does not occur in the Bible and has not yet been traced to any Rabbinical source. 'And remember Our servant Job when he cried unto his Lord, "Verily Satan hath laid on me disease and pain." "Stamp," said We, "with thy foot. This to wash with, cool, and to drink"' (xxxviii, vv. 40–3). The commentators say that it was the angel Gabriel who was sent to deliver this message to Job, and he lifted the afflicted Prophet up from the ground

[1] Plate XII.

where he was lying in misery and dejection. This incident is pictured in the MS. of the *Stories of the Prophets* (fol. 159 b) belonging to Mr. Chester Beatty.

There is a story in the Qur'ān (ii, *v.* 261) which the Muslim commentators connect with the Prophet Jeremiah, though it seems rather to be based upon Ezekiel's vision of the Valley of Dry Bones, or on the story of the scepticism of Esdras as to the possibility of the rebuilding of Jerusalem after its destruction by Nebuchadnezzar. The passage in the Qur'ān tells of a man 'who passed by a city which had been laid in ruins. "How," said he, "shall God give life to this city after it had been dead?" And God caused him to die for a hundred years and then raised him to life and said, "How long hast thou waited?" He said, "I have waited a day or part of a day." He said, "Nay thou hast waited a hundred years. Look on thy food and thy drink; they are not corrupted; and look on thine ass; We will make thee a sign unto men; and look on the bones how We join them together, then clothe them with flesh." And when this was shown to him he said, "I acknowledge that God hath power to do all things." ' This picture is taken from the MS. of Rashīd ud-Dīn's *Universal History* (A.D. 1310) in the Edinburgh University Library,[1] and is typical of the profound melancholy which is a distinguishing feature of most of the illustrations in this MS. The Prophet appears to receive no encouragement from the sight of his ass, which has already recovered part of its flesh and skin, though its hind limbs are still skeleton.

This completes our survey of the Old Testament. The New Testament will form the subject of the next lecture.

[1] Plate XIII.

PLATE XIII

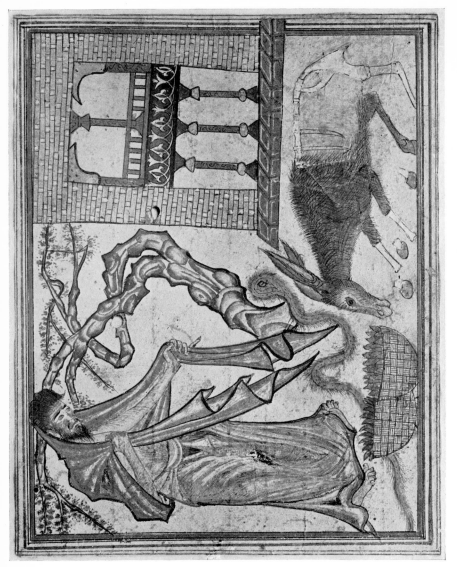

JEREMIAH (?)

CHAPTER III

MUḤAMMAD'S knowledge of the New Testament appears to have been much more limited than his knowledge of the Old, for the only personages whose names he mentions are Zacharias, St. John the Baptist, the Virgin Mary, and Jesus. The accounts of these found in the Qur'ān can only partially be traced back to the Gospels and are in larger measure derived from Apocryphal writings. The chapter (xix) entitled 'Mary' begins with an account of the prayer of Zacharias in the Temple and the announcement that a son would be born to him, but the sign of dumbness that falls upon him lasts only for three nights instead of several months, as in the Gospel narrative. Of the preaching of St. John the Baptist no account whatsoever is given, and the only incident of his life mentioned is that of his birth.

The Virgin Mary is first mentioned when, before her birth, her mother says, 'O my Lord, I vow to Thee what is in my womb for Thy special service. Accept it from me, for Thou hearest and knowest.' And when she had given birth to it, she said, 'O my Lord, verily I have brought forth a female, and I have named her Mary, and I take refuge with Thee for her, and for her offspring, from Satan the stoned' (iii, *v.* 31). Mary is brought up in the Temple, where Zacharias finds her miraculously supplied with food, as described in the apocryphal gospel of the Nativity.

A little farther on in the same chapter comes the account of the Annunciation. 'When the Angel said, "O Mary, Verily God announceth to thee a Word from Him; his name shall be Messiah, Jesus the Son of Mary, illustrious in this world and in the next, and one of those who have near access to God; and He shall speak to men alike when in the cradle and when grown-up; and He shall be one of the just"' (iii, *vv.* 40, 41).

The account of the Nativity differs from that given in the

F

Gospel, in that it is not described as taking place in a stable, but by the trunk of a palm tree in a remote and desolate place.

We have recognized in the previous lectures how frequently the Muhammadan artist, having no guidance from the theologian of his own creed, has had recourse to Christian art for his delineation of the Christian story. I have already shown that this was the case in connexion with a Muhammadan picture of the Annunciation; but such imitation was not possible in the case of a Muhammadan picture of the Nativity, since the account given in the Qur'ān differs so fundamentally from that in the Gospel narrative. Accordingly, the Muslim artist had to create his own type and reconstruct the scene out of his own imagination. The only known example of such a Muhammadan representation of the Nativity is that in a MS. of the *Stories of the Prophets*, dating from the end of the sixteenth century, now in the possession of Mr. Chester Beatty.[1]

Certain of the miracles of Jesus are mentioned in the Qur'ān, such as the healing of the blind and of the lepers, and the raising of the dead, and a miracle, mentioned also in the apocryphal gospel of the Infancy, according to which Jesus makes the figure of a bird out of clay, and when He breathes into it, it becomes a living bird (iii, *v*. 43). One of the miracles recorded seems to be a confusion of the Last Supper and the feeding of the five thousand. The account given in the Qur'ān (in the chapter called 'The Table') is as follows:

'Remember when the apostles said, "O Jesus, Son of Mary, is thy Lord able to send down a furnished table to us out of heaven?" He said, "Fear God, if ye be believers." They said, "We desire to eat therefrom and to have our hearts assured; and to know that thou hast indeed spoken truth to us and to be witnesses thereof." Jesus, Son of Mary, said, "O God our Lord, send down a table to us out of heaven, that it may become a recurring festival to us, to the first of us and to the last of us, and a sign from Thee; and do

[1] Qiṣa al-Anbiyā, fol. 225; see Plate XIV.

PLATE XIV

THE NATIVITY

PLATE XV

THE LAST SUPPER

PLATE XVI

THE BAPTISM

Thou nourish us, for Thou art the best of nourishers." And God said, "Verily I will cause it to descend unto you" ' (v, *vv.* 112–15).

The commentators offer a variety of details in their exposition of this miracle, but the most received tradition is that in response to the prayer of Jesus, God sent down from Heaven a table, on which was a fish ready dressed, without tail or prickly fins, dropping with fat and having salt at its head and vinegar at its tail, and round it various kinds of herbs, together with five loaves of bread, on one of which there were olives; on the second honey; on the third butter; on the fourth cheese; and on the fifth dried flesh. This would seem to be the source of the picture which occurs in the MS. of Mīrkhwānd's *History* in the Bibliothèque Nationale (Suppl. persan 1567, fol. 163).[1] This picture dates from the seventeenth century, but has characteristics which suggest that it is a copy of a work of the sixteenth. The fish is seen lying on a flat dish or table with what looks like three pomegranates in front of it. The artist has put in six loaves, though the text he is illustrating clearly says five only, and he has added little platters which apparently contain the various ingredients said by the commentators to be lying on the loaves. This is the only Muhammadan picture known which in the remotest degree approximates to a representation of the Last Supper.

As the Qur'ān denies the Crucifixion of Jesus, maintaining that the Jews crucified in His place some one who was made to appear like unto Him (iv, *v.* 156), Muhammadan art lacks any pictures of the Crucifixion, for which it could have found so many models in Christian art.

The Qur'ān makes no mention of the baptism of Jesus, but a picture of it occurs in the MS. already referred to of al-Beruni's great work on various systems of chronology in the world, now in the Edinburgh University Library (No. 161, fol. 165 b).[2] The artistic provenance of this picture is very uncertain, and until we know more about the pictorial

[1] Plate XV.   [2] Plate XVI.

art of this early period, for the MS. bears the date A.H. 707 (A.D. 1307–8), it can be only a matter of speculation.

Similarly it was left to the later Muhammadan historians of the Lives of the Prophets to bring in any mention of the Temptation, to which there is no reference in the Qur'ān. In the same MS. of Mīrkhwānd's *History* so often referred to,[1] Jesus is represented as casting a stone at the Devil, and we have here one of the very few attempts to represent the Devil, for in Muhammadan painting he is by no means so familiar a figure as in Christian art.

Another picture of about the same date[2] represents the Virgin Mary seated under a palm tree with the Child Jesus on her knee. This picture is remarkable in that the Virgin has the flame halo which in Muslim art usually indicates a Prophet, though she is never reckoned among the Prophets of Islam.

As in the case of other great personages of sacred history, the Muslim commentators and compilers of histories of the Prophets considerably amplified the narration as set forth in the Qur'ān. The poets also, especially those who wrote with a didactic or mystical purpose, incorporated in their poems many stories of Jesus, some of which derive their origin from the Gospel. Thus the well-known poet Sa'dī has introduced into his *Būstān* a story which is obviously an echo of the parable of the Pharisee and the Publican. Jesus is said to have been one day in the company of a devout person, when a reprobate, overhearing their conversation, repented him of his evil way and resolved to amend his life. So in profound humility he draws near to the two holy personages, but the devout ascetic, annoyed at the interruption, wishes harshly to drive him away. Whereupon Jesus rebukes him in much the same spirit as in the Gospel narrative He expresses His commendation of the Publican.[3]

[1] Bibliothèque Nationale (Suppl. persan 1565, fol. 155 b).

[2] Bibliothèque Nationale (Suppl. persan 1313, fol. 174).

[3] See *Painting in Islam*, plate XXVI, and for other paintings of Jesus, ibid., plates XXVII and XXVIII.

It is of interest to note that the Muslim artists never worked out a distinctive type in their representations of Jesus. He is commonly made to appear in the form and dress of such a holy person as the painter may have seen among his own contemporaries. As Jesus was specially distinguished among the Prophets of Islam as being the only one among them who never married, the Muslim artist sometimes portrayed Him as a dervish, and gave Him the form of one of the ascetics of his own time and country, who had renounced all the pleasures and attractions of the world. One of the earliest examples of such a type occurs in a MS. dated 1388.[1] In a much later Turkish picture painted towards the close of the seventeenth century, we see Jesus seated bare-headed on the ground in the humble attitude of the Muslim devotee.[2] The picture occurs in an illustrated genealogical tree of the Sultans of Turkey, to which is prefixed the genealogy of the Prophets and the Patriarchs. It appears to be a copy of an earlier composition of the same kind made in the reign of Sulayman the Magnificent (*ob.* 1566), and the portraits are probably also copies, so that this conception of Jesus may well be the work of a Turkish painter of the sixteenth century, though in the present MS. the genealogy has been continued to the reign of Sultan Muḥammad IV, who came to the throne in 1687.

In a MS. dated 1650 we find another entirely different type. Jesus walks through the bazaar of a town in Northern Persia in the ordinary habit of a simple devotee, and his disciples who accompany him appear like the townfolk whom the painter saw every day around him.

To a later period—sometime in the eighteenth century —belongs an entirely different Persian representation, in which Jesus is seen talking to a shepherd. This picture occurs as an illustration in a MS. of Jalāl ud-Dīn's *Mathnawī*, a work which might have been expected to provide abundant

---

[1] Bibliothèque Nationale (Suppl. persan 3321, fol. 233 b).

[2] Subhat al-Akhbār, fol. 8 (A.F. 50 (143), Nationalbibliothek, Wien, plate XXIX); see *Painting in Islam*, plate XXIX.

material for the painter to exercise his talent upon, filled as it is with numerous stories attractively and often dramatically told. But it was probably the religious character of this work which stood in the way of its being placed in the hand of the painter. Another example of the Muslim painter's desire to present this holy personage in a form that would appear intelligible to his fellow-countrymen is given in a MS. of Afghan poetry, bearing the date 1873; here Jesus is represented in the guise of such a religious teacher as was familiar to the Afghan artist in his own times, and under similar circumstances, seated on the upper terrace of a house, conversing with two devout inquirers, who kneel humbly before him, one a man and the other a woman.[1]

From the artistic point of view, these pictures are decidedly unattractive; their importance lies in their significance for religious history. The very fact that in no single instance is there any attempt made to copy any Christian representation of the figure of Jesus is based on the Muhammadan conviction that Jesus was theirs—that he was a Prophet of Islam—and that he did not belong to the rival religion that called itself after his name. From the standpoint of Christian art and of the long story of Christian achievement, we are tempted to regard any Muhammadan utterances about Jesus as borrowings. But we must remember that the Muslim derived his knowledge of Jesus and his conception of his personality and nature from the Qur'ān, which according to Islamic doctrine is the Word of God, co-eternal with God, and communicated both in language and meaning, through divine inspiration, to the last of the Prophets, Muḥammad. In so far as the Muhammadans claimed to have any knowledge of Jesus beyond the record they found in the Qur'ān, such supplementary information they owed to the Traditions of Muḥammad, which, according to the Muslim theologians, were, so far as their meaning and content were concerned, derived from the same divine

[1] Bibliothèque Nationale (Suppl. persan 991, fol. 56); see Plate XVII.

PLATE XVII

JESUS IN AFGHAN DRESS

source as the Qur'ān itself, though the actual wording of these Traditions was not held to have been similarly inspired. The Muhammadans felt no need to go to Christian sources for information regarding Jesus—similarly in the world of art they elected to devise a type of their own.

In the historical period with which we are now concerned, we have gone far beyond those early beginnings of Muslim religious painting, in which help was sought from Christian artists; in the years that followed the long-drawn-out conflict of the Crusades, and the overbearing attitude of the oriental Christians towards their Muhammadan fellow-subjects in the earlier period of the Mongol conquest, when the new rulers were still heathen, there was a growing bitterness between the Christian and the Islamic world, and it is quite possible that this bitterness stood in the way of the admittance into Muslim religious art of any specifically Christian representation of a holy personage, in regard to whom so much controversy had raged between the adherents of the two rival faiths, around whose personality had grown up the doctrines which formed the main distinguishing lines of division between Christianity and Islam.

Accordingly, the Muhammadan artists devised for themselves representations of Jesus, which made him out to be one of themselves, and avoided introducing into their own art any Christian type. In a similar spirit, we find a Turkish painter dressing up Zacharias and St. John the Baptist like Turks,[1] though the picture of the Virgin Mary, set by the side of them, is clearly copied from an Italian original. These pictures are taken from a late Turkish MS. of the eighteenth century, of a history of the world. But, speaking generally, during the earlier centuries of Muslim art, after the primitive Christian influences had ceased to be operative, we find no distinctive fixed type either for Jesus or for the Virgin Mary, nor is there any such convention in regard to costume as recurs again in different periods of Christian art through successive centuries. For the Muslim artist generally repre-

[1] See *Painting in Islam*, plate XXIX.

sents the Virgin in the dress that was familiar to him in his own country. This is noticeable in the two pictures of the sixteenth century, which I have already shown you. In both of these, the Muhammadan artist apparently worked without guidance from any external source, apart from the artistic influences of his own time and country. But the advent of Christian missionaries into the Muhammadan East, especially in connexion with the efforts made in the sixteenth century by the Portuguese to extend their power in the Oriental world, introduced a new interest and a new type of representation.

These missionaries brought with them a number of pictures representing devotional subjects. These were much admired in India, and we find them pasted into albums along with examples of some of the finest specimens of indigenous art. For instance, cheap woodcuts, obviously regarded as rare treasures, are found in the Jahāngīr album in the State Library, Berlin, and in the Dārā Shikoh album in the India Office Library. Sometimes Muhammadan artists were set to work to copy these engravings. It is clear that the nature of the process of their production was not understood and that they were regarded as actual pen drawings, and were valued in comparison with specimens of the calligraphic art to which Muhammadan connoisseurs attached so high a value. Consequently we find that the Oriental artist sometimes tried to imitate these engravings under the impression that they were original examples of minute line work. On the other hand, it is seldom that any attempt is made to copy them exactly, for in the majority of cases the pictures undergo in the process various modifications intended to adapt them to Oriental taste; not only is the original design considerably altered, but a wood engraving is sometimes changed into a coloured picture and set in an elaborate coloured border filled with figures of various kinds.

Towards the latter part of the sixteenth century such pictures of the Virgin Mary became increasingly popular in the Muhammadan world, especially in India. The impulse in this direction came from the Jesuit fathers, Ridolfo Aquaviva and Antonio Monserrate, who visited the court of Akbar in 1580. They brought with them a number of books and pictures, among which was a copy of the picture of the Virgin Mary attributed to St. Luke, now over the altar in the Borghese chapel in the church of Santa Maria Maggiore in Rome.[1] The emperor is said to have regarded these pictures with profound veneration, and when he visited the oratory of the fathers, to have shown great reverence for the pictures of Jesus and the Virgin Mary, and to have ordered his own painters to make copies of those which the fathers had placed in their chapel.[2] Even after the Jesuits in 1583 had left the Mughal court, realizing the ill-success of their mission, Akbar determined in 1590 to celebrate the Feast of the Assumption in his own fashion, and 'caused a high throne to be erected, upon which he placed the picture of the Blessed Virgin which Father Ridolfo had given to him, commanding all his princes, captains, and courtiers to do it reverence, and to kiss it. The chief lords of the court demanded that the eldest son of the king should first set them the example, and this he at once and very willingly did. The most distinguished of the officers showed themselves the readiest to honour the Virgin'.[3]

Though such behaviour was certainly unusual in a Muhammadan monarch, yet the Jesuit fathers had not sufficient warrant for interpreting it as indicating attach-ment to the Christian faith, when they wrote that 'it seemed to be the will of Our Saviour to rouse this great monarch from his sleep of obstinacy, and to inspire him to emerge from the shades of unbelief into the light of the true faith, and to spread the same throughout his kingdom. This, we may without impiety believe, was through the

---

[1] *Akbar and the Jesuits: An Account of the Jesuit Missions to the Court of Akbar,* by Father Pierre du Jarric, S.J. Translated by C. H. Payne (London, 1926), pp. 19–20.   [2] Id., p. 26.   [3] Id., p. 44.

intercession of the Blessed Virgin Mary, towards whom this Prince had always been powerfully attracted'.[1]

In coming to this conclusion the Jesuit fathers had forgotten the high place which Islamic theology assigns to the Virgin Mary. In the Qur'ān she is described as ever-virgin (lxvi, *v.* 12) and as 'she who kept her maidenhood and into whom We breathed of Our spirit' (xxi, *v.* 91). In Chapter iii, *v.* 37, we read, 'And the angel said, "O Mary, God hath chosen thee, and purified thee, and chosen thee above the women of the world."' Thus from the outset, Muḥammad taught the virginity of Mary, and there is reason for thinking also Her immaculate conception. One of the traditions assigned to him declares that every new-born child has been touched by Satan with the exception of Mary and Jesus. If therefore it be accepted that religious pictures should be admitted into the devotional practices of Islam, as was undoubtedly the opinion of Akbar, it would appear that his reverent behaviour was entirely in accordance with orthodox Muslim belief.

The interest which Akbar took in the pictures which the Christian missionaries brought to his court received permanent memorial in the fresco which still remains on the walls of one of his palaces in Fathpur-Sikri. It occurs in the so-called House of Miriam, the residence of one of his Hindu queens, the daughter of Raja Bihari Mall, the chief of Amber or, as it is now called, Jaipur, in Rajputana. This lady was the mother of the future emperor Jahāngīr and she received as her posthumous official title Maryam-zamānī, that is, the Mary of the Age. This fresco represents a winged figure seated on a chair with a high back, and wearing a long flowing robe caught up over the left arm, which rests upon the breast hidden by a blue tippet. Opposite is an angel, the outline of whose face and wings are now only traceable. There seems good reason for accepting the local tradition which declares this fresco to be a representation of the Annunciation, and if this is correct

[1] Id., p. 44.

the fact that the artist has represented the Virgin with wings must be regarded as an addition created out of his individual fantasy.

The Emperor Jahāngīr never manifested the same interest in the study of religion as did his father, but he remained in friendly relations with the Jesuit missionaries, except during the earlier part of his reign, and the religious policy which he generally followed was one of toleration. The Jesuit relation gives a long account of the Christian pictures which Jahāngīr caused to be painted in his palaces in Agra. On the ceiling of one room was a picture of Christ surrounded by angels, while on the walls were some saints in miniature, such as St. John the Baptist, St. Anthony, and others, as well as some women saints. Above the window (*jharokha*) in which the emperor was seated when he showed himself to the people, in accordance with the daily custom of the Mughal emperors, was, on one side, a picture of Christ holding the orb in His hand, and on the other a copy of the painting of the Virgin Mary taken from the picture which the Jesuit fathers had given to Akbar, a copy of the painting in the Borghese Chapel, attributed to St. Luke. Inside the window also, on the vaulted roof of the balcony, were similar pictures of Christ and the Virgin Mary. The Jesuit relation speaks of the gratification which the sight of these pictures caused to the Jesuit fathers, whenever they had audience of this emperor, and of the scandal which the presence of them in such a place excited in the minds of the Muhammadans. For, it was said, it looked more like the verandah of a pious and Catholic king than that of a Moor. In the interior of Jahāngīr's palaces also there were pictures representing the mysteries of Christ and scenes from the lives of the Apostles. The emperor personally selected the subjects which were to be copied, probably from the European woodcuts which the Jesuits had given him, and he would send his painters to the fathers, in order that they might ascertain what particular colours they were to use for the garments of each figure. The Jesuit narrator adds:

'This is a painful eyesore to the Moors, for they are so averse to pictures that they do not suffer to be represented those of their own faith whom they look upon as saints, much less those of the Christian faith which they so much dislike.' It would take too long here to repeat in detail the various accounts that the Jesuits gave of individual pictures which were presented to Jahāngīr and which he invariably had copied by his court painters.

The emperor even went so far as to cause the great tomb which he had erected in memory of his father at Sikandra, a little way outside the city of Agra, to be decorated with frescoes, and fortunately Manucci, though with some difficulty, managed to get sight of them before the emperor Aurangzeb ordered them to be obliterated with whitewash. As is well known, the tomb of Akbar stands in the middle of a vast park, surrounded by a lofty wall built of red sandstone. In the principal gateway leading into this enclosure, Manucci saw a picture of Christ on the Cross, another of the Virgin Mary, and another of St. Ignatius. On the ceiling of the vast dome above the grave of Akbar were great angels and cherubim and many other painted figures.[1]

Of none of these pictures does a single trace remain, but fortunately some slight indication of their nature is preserved in some of the pictures of Jahāngīr's period, for example in one of the pictures in the Wantage collection now in the Indian Museum, representing Nur Jahān entertaining Jahāngīr and Prince Khurram, in 1617, where we find reproduced just such pictures as the Jesuit fathers saw on either side of the *jharokha*, the Virgin Mary and Christ holding the orb in His hand.[2]

Also, in the well-known picture of the Durbar of Jahāngīr formerly in the possession of Dr. Schulz (now in the Museum of Fine Arts, Boston), just above the head of the emperor is clearly visible a picture of the Virgin which was possibly intended to be a copy of the painting attributed to St. Luke,

[1] N. Manucci, *Storia de Mogor*, translated by William Irvine (London, 1907), vol. i, p. 141. [2] Plate XVIII.

PLATE XVIII

CHRISTIAN PAINTINGS IN THE
PALACE OF JAHĀNGĪR

PLATE XIX

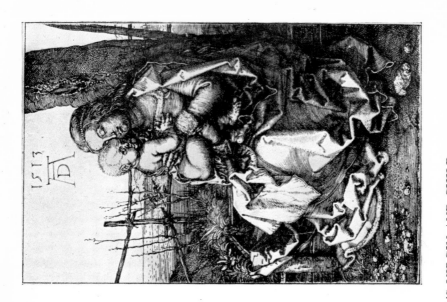

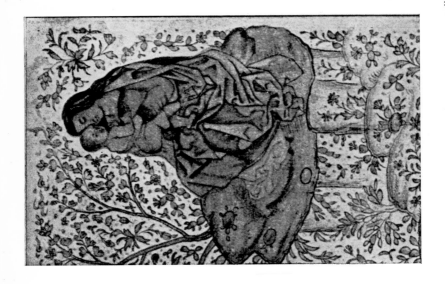

INDIAN COPY OF DÜRER'S VIRGIN AND CHILD

in the Borghese chapel in Rome, while on the other side of
the canopy is a kneeling figure, behind which is an angel
that may well have formed part of a picture of the Crucifixion.

It has been found possible to identify some of the Christian pictures copied into royal albums from European woodcuts, especially wood engravings printed in Antwerp at the
close of the sixteenth century. These Indian imitators
showed their good taste by being especially attracted by the
work of Albrecht Dürer, though of course they must have
been quite ignorant of his work generally or even of his
name. In Jahāngīr's Album in Berlin, we find a copy of the
St. John who stands at the foot of the Cross in a Crucifixion
which Dürer drew in 1511; but the Indian artist has slightly
changed the pose of the head, and made the Apostle look
in the opposite direction. Still further liberties have been
taken with a Virgin and Child which Dürer drew in 1513,
but the source of the Indian painting is unmistakable.[1] In
other cases an attempt is made to copy the original exactly,
as in the case of a Holy Family painted by Johann Rotten-
hamer (1564–1623), an engraving of which was published
in 1601; here the Indian painter has introduced very little
of his own, but apparently he considered the foliage of the
tree to be too thick, and he has omitted the basket in the
corner, which was probably of a kind unfamiliar to him,
and has sprinkled the foreground with flowers, in a manner
common in Persian and Indian pictures.

In Persia at a much later date there was a recrudescence
of this fashion for pictures of Christian religious subjects,
and in the eighteenth century there grew up an active
school of such painters, the most distinguished representative of whom was Āghā Shāh Najaf, who flourished in the
reign of Karīm Khān Zand (1750–79) and lived on into
the nineteenth century. A favourite subject was the Holy
Family, with attendant angels, and these pictures were
painted on the backs of hand-mirrors or on the lids of toilet-

[1] Plate XIX.

boxes, and the colouring, dress, and grouping of the figures clearly indicate that they are imitated from European paintings, generally French.

As in India in the latter years of the sixteenth century and the beginning of the seventeenth century, this taste for Christian religious pictures imported from the West must not be taken to connote any particular attraction towards the Christian faith. It indicates an artistic fashion merely, stimulated largely by the novelty of the foreign importations. The lack of genuine religious feeling is revealed by the frivolous and unedifying character of the other paintings commonly found in juxtaposition to these religious pictures.

This completes all I have to say regarding the Old and the New Testaments in Muhammadan art. I cannot claim to have made anything like a complete survey of the subject, especially as the requisite materials still remain hidden away in the Oriental collections of widely scattered libraries, which have hitherto been very little explored. There is no doubt that much still remains for future investigators to discover. Nor, on the other hand, have the narrow limits of my subject allowed me to touch upon more than a very small part of the vast field of Islamic religious art which is concerned with subjects other than those drawn from the Old and the New Testaments. Such examples of illustrations of subjects taken from the Old and New Testaments as I have put before you cannot, I fear, claim to take any high rank in the history of painting, in consideration of any artistic merit they may possess. They belong for the most part, with the notable exception of the story of Joseph, to a class of subject which did not secure for them a place in the luxuriously decorated MSS. which formed part of the treasures in royal libraries in the Muhammadan East. For these Bible stories found no mention in the Shāh Nāmah of Firdawsī, and but little in the Khamsah of Nizāmī or the poems of Sa'di, or in such other works, to the decoration of which the great artists who enjoyed the patronage of these Muhammadan princes were called upon to devote their talents. Consequently on hardly any of the illustrations which I have put before you do we find inscribed any of the great names in the annals of either Persian, Indian, or Turkish art. The reason is possibly to be found in the widespread condemnation of representational art in the Muslim world, and this hostile attitude would in double measure find expression in regard to such attempts to depict the holy personages of sacred history. The interest, therefore, of these pictures consists largely in the evidence they afford of the refusal of artistic tradition to give way before the attacks of ecclesiastical authorities, and the insight they give into the psychology of the Muslim peoples in the various historical periods in which they made their appearance.